B IS FOR BREATHE

The ABCs of Coping with Fussy and Frustrating Feelings

By Dr. Melissa Munro Boyd

Printed in the United States of America
First Edition, 2019

ISBN 978-0-692-18983-2

This Book is Dedicated to

My husband Bryan and our Big 3-
Bryanna, Bryan Jr., and Bryson

Thank you for loving me and teaching me.

When you are feeling Fussy or Frustrated
And want something to do
Try a new coping skill
One of these will surely help you

A is for ART

B is for BREATHE

C is for COUNT to 10

D is for DANCE

E is for EAT a healthy snack

F is for FUN with a Friend

G is for create a GLITTER jar

H is for HUG a trusted person

I is for IMAGINE a favorite place

J is for tell JOKES

K is for KICK a ball and play other sports

L is for LISTEN to music

M is for MUSCLE relaxation

N is for NATURE walk

O is for ORGANIZE and clean up toys

P is for PRAY

Q is for QUIET time

R is for READ

S is for positive SELF-talk

T is for TALK about feelings

U is for UNPLUG

V is for VISION board

W is for WRITE about feelings

X is for play the XYLOPHONE and other musical instruments

Y is for YOGA

Z is for ZZZ (rest)

Draw or paint to help express emotions

B is for BREATHE

Breathe by slowly taking a deep breath in through your nose and slowly breathing out through your mouth

C is for COUNT TO 10

Slowly count to 10 while thinking about feeling calm

Express pleasure through motion

Good food choices are healthy for the mind and body

Enjoy an activity with a friend, like playing a game

Use water, glitter, glue, food coloring-
Make, Shake, Watch and Relax as glitter settles)

A caring hug from a trusted family/friend is comforting

I is for IMAGINE a favorite place

Imagine your favorite calm and relaxing
place in your mind, such as a beach

I is for tell JOKES

Laughing and telling jokes helps to relax

K is for KICK a ball
and play other sports

Physical activity relieves stress and builds self-esteem

L is for LISTEN to music

Listen to a favorite song, ocean waves,
waterfalls or birds

Slowly tense and then relax each muscle
group- face, hands, arms, stomach, legs, feet)

Enjoy walking while focusing on senses
and nature around you

O is for ORGANIZE
and clean up toys

Cleaning up and clearing out clutter is calming

Prayer can help bring peace to your mind and body

Enjoy the quiet and focus attention on the present

R is for READ

Reading relaxes your mind

Positive self-talk helps to boost feelings
and self-esteem

Share feelings and talk with a trusted person
to help feel better

Take a break from electronics to relax the mind

V is for create a VISION board

Create pictures and words to express feelings
and think of future goals

W is for WRITE about feelings

Journal to express emotions, communicate feelings, and solve problems

Enjoy playing a musical instrument that is joyful and fun

Yoga relaxes the mind and releases tension in the body

Get Good Rest and Take a Break to help relax emotions

Made in the USA
Middletown, DE
16 March 2019